A Young Man's Ravings on New America

By

K.C. Stone

Table of Contents

A Brief Introduction and My Thoughts on the State of Things

I am death writing about life. I am hate singing about love. I am apathy raving about enthusiasm. Lastly, and perhaps worst of all, I am young speaking of what it means to be old. I am of a generation that came of age during a time of over the top, gratuitous violence. That low-down kind of violence that nags at you when you try to sleep. The kind of violence that, once witnessed, may never be un-seen. That sort of horrible, gut wrenching, heart throbbing, throat spewing, soul numbing violence that tore down the confidences of each and every American that once loved and believed in their country when they witnessed the death of two towers.

With us comes the end of the American century. With us comes the end of everything that traditionally made someone a member of this country. Gone are the days of American exceptionalism. Gone are the days of needless expansion. Gone are the days of unwavering patriotism and the feeling of uninhibited freedom that (judging on what I've read of those times) seemed to invade every corner of this once great nation. Even before I got a chance to experience it, the mighty Wild West had been tamed.

I was young and impressionable during a time where people, my very own parents even, would openly mock and scoff at their leaders in Washington as if they were all bumbling buffoons frequently appearing on television to stumble dumbly over their words and spew clear bullshit at us as if we all were too stupid to see through it. The thing that always struck me most in those days was that there were some people who were that stupid, and would gobble that shit up as if they were hippos who were all too hungry hungry for bullshit. I was young and impressionable during a time where you were only a right wing Republican or a left-wing Democrat and there was nothing in-between besides bomb shells and crossfire that absolutely no one wanted to get caught up in. People still give me odd looks when I explain to them that my political mind-set is a blend of both ideologies, and I always have to ask at the end if it makes sense or if they understand.

For a whole half a century, we devoted most of our efforts to combating the scourge of Communism, or, as most modern Americans know it, that pretentious, youthful rebellion of an ideology that's only there for hipsters in their early twenties who want to feel intellectually superior to all of the Capitalist adults that have run their economy into the ground. Hell, I was even a Communist for a time, an Anarcho-Communist even, as a result of a brief rage against the American machine for imposing its morality on me with handcuffs. Nowadays, we're fighting the same battle only against a different enemy. Ever since the attacks on New York City in 2001, we've been fighting a "War on Terror" throughout the globe, and I can only assume that it's a battle that will only be won once the very feeling of terror is erased from the slate of possible emotions a human is capable of feeling. Men and women my age went overseas to attempt to fight a war of ideologies with blood. One cannot fight a war of the mind like a war of the body, else one is willing to fight until the end of time, or until each and every person on this planet is eradicated as a result. It makes me sad that we seemed so willing to do both.

Poetry

Worship the Sun

I'm standing
On a grassy hill
In the middle
Of the suburbs.

Breathlessly,
I stare at the sun
Shooting its mighty
White rays
Upon the Earth
And all its people
As they go about their lives
On this particular day.

If I could pick
One God
To call the master of all things,
I would choose the Sun.
I come to this conclusion
As I watch
The light invade every corner
Formerly dark,
Exposing
And making naked
Everything that was previously hidden

By hideous black.
I come to this conclusion
As I watch
The sleeping Earth
Come to life
Once my Lord
Decides it's time to get up.

As the day presses on,
He grows brighter
And hotter,
As if he's angry
At his children
For ignoring him
For so long.

His children
His children
Just march on,
Putting their faith
In other Gods
Who never had the guts
To show their faces
As he does.

His children

His children

Just march on,

Taking for granted

The gift

Of light.

Eventually,

After a day of pleading

His children

To notice him,

Our Lord becomes tired,

And grows quieter

Until, finally, he gives up altogether,

And falls utterly silent,

Allowing the darkness

To swarm

And descend upon his loves.

To terrorize them

And blind them

And trick them into sin.

In this silence,

I notice that the neighborhood

Has gone dark

And fallen asleep to the song

The moon was barely chanting

From up above.

I press
A cigarette to my lips
And light the tip,
A stick of tobacco with God at the end,
And walk leisurely to my own bed
So I may be well rested for tomorrow
To worship my Lord again.

I Made You a Home

I thought
That if I built you a mountain,
You could climb
To its peak
And look down
On the world below you,
And roll marbles down its face
Just to see if you could trip up all the climbers.

I'm told
That when you're all the way
Up there,

The air becomes clear

And full of calm.

The wind whispers lullabies;

You can hold clouds in your palm.

You could

Separate yourself

From the humidity and loss

Of the ground

Below you.

Or, so I thought.

Once you got to the top,

You found the cold

Unbearable.

Not to mention it was a bitch getting up.

You were disappointed

To find it was just as tough

Getting down,

Let alone to adjust.

So, I dug you a pit

And made you a home.

The air was thick

And drenched with cleansing.

You could drown your woe in steam.

I thought

Its warmth would be inviting

And that, although you're steeped deeply

Within its constant rumblings,

You could stand steady and alright,

Though your world

Is so unstable.

But, you found it too stuffy

And dirty

And hot.

So, I let you alone

So you could find your own home.

Something I guess

I should have done from the start.

It's only up to you

Where you choose to place your heart.

You chose a quiet little patch

Of prairie

On the edge of a wood,

And made you a life

Just as best as you could.

And your best was good enough.

In the summer,

The air was warm

And the Earth was buzzing with life.

Come winter,

The chill brought a calm

As the world slept around you.

And you loved the transitions between the two.

I thought if I built you a mountain,

You'd learn to love the cold.

I thought if I dug you a ditch,

You would learn to love the heat.

It never occurred to me that you'd need both.

The Poet

"There it is, behind you."

He said

And he pointed to the door

Behind her.

"Leave if you'd like."

She stared

For a while

At him,

Probing his face to determine

If he was serious.

He was.

Her heart broken,

She left his house wordlessly

Without a glance back

To make it

Easy.

"Finally, I'm free!"

The man rejoiced

To himself.

He finally had

The peace and quiet

He had been hoping for

For months on end

So he could get back to his writing

And the things that interest him

Without worrying

About her constant needs

And wants

And fears

And thoughts.

He was with himself now.

All alone was he.

To him

There was no “her”,

No more “we”

To him,

All that was left

Was “me”.

He turned to his desk

To press pen to paper

And, in his new found freedom,

Write the most magnificent,

Socially relevant poem

He had ever written.

But, as the tip
Hit the sheet,
He found
That he could procure no words.

He would start on a work
Over and over again,
Never satisfied with the roads
He was attempting to explore
And crumple the poem
To be thrown out
With the rest of the trash.

"No words!"
He thought,
"What could be worse!"
He felt as though
Without any words,
He was without a soul.

And he was.

He gave up
For the night,

And retired himself
To some drink,
Some dark,
Dark whiskey
That burned the back of his throat
Like bleach
On bare skin.

Now drunk,
He laid himself
In his bed
To look up at the ceiling
In darkness
And in silence
That seemed to consume
His very being
And chip away
At his
Unfeeling veneer
To expose his fragile core
To the harshness
Of the night.

He was not used to this
For he always

Had her

To stay close to him

On nights like these,

Like a protective coating

Of love

Against the dangers

Of indifference

And eventual

Despair.

He began to wonder

About her:

Where she could be,

What she could be doing,

Who she was with.

And a sadness

Seeped into his bones

From the dark

As if through some

Sinister osmosis,

And he thought about

Going to look for her.

But

He knew this was futile.

He knew she could be anywhere
Under the great big
Black
American sky.

That American sky
That watches dreamers
Become dust,
Eroded by the winds
Of cynicism.

That American sky
That rains coldly
On warm,
Summer afternoons
To drive the children
Back indoors,
To brood
And watch their playthings
Sit sadly
In the storm.

That American sky
That stretches endlessly
Across continents,

Ignoring borders
And dissent
To claim land for its own.

That American sky
That laughs at him now
For wanting to chase
Elusive specters,
Ghosts he used to love,
Like the dream
It always promised him
Since he was a boy.

Dissatisfaction
Runs deep
In the veins of those who chase
That deep blue American sky,
As it always has been,
And always will be.

Thus is the American way,
That when we find
That which satisfies, and loves us most,
We are so prone to point to the door behind it
And ask it nicely

To leave.

An Endless Wailing

Worse men than I

Have come,

Century after century,

Millenia after millennia,

They have come to say the exact same things

That I have come to say to you,

Only, they said it better.

Like bitter teeth

Wailing against a brick wall,

Their musings grow forward

And up

Beside a forgotten wasteland

Of cheap liquor

And disease ridden,

Boisterous

Low lifes

That make slums of rolling

Hill tops.

Seething with

Over-whelming rage

And Tragically trapped in the toils

Of solitude,

May we walk endlessly,

Or until our feet begin to rot

And fall off,

Toe by toe,

Bone by rotten bone,

Making skeletons

Of old Roman emperors

And Indian chiefs

That paved the way for greatness

We assume we have followed.

The night

Doesn’t take kindly

To those who can’t stand the cold.

And I,

Being one who chose to wear

Open toed,

Flimsy sandals,

Barely enough to keep my feet warm in the summer time,

Am one of those people.

It has not been just once

That I've stumbled aimlessly

In places unfamiliar to me

From light time

To darkness,

Wanting to sleep

Or find shelter

Or find shelter to sleep,

Stoned and alone.

It has not been just once

That I've lusted for life beyond my means

And beyond my ambition,

Which seems to impede the dusk

And anchor our lives

To the seemingly bottomless,

Soulless pit

Of lonely Suburbia.

O lonely Suburbia!

O lonely suburbia!

You have wrapped me

In your plastic arms,

Never to decompose for several lifetimes.

You have watched me grow up
Into a perfectly respectable,
Perfectly polite
Young man.
And a YOUNG man
I am.

O Suburbia!
O sweet suburbia!
If you would take me,
If you would have me,
Please,
Do not hesitate to cradle me to sleep
In the residential
Slaughterhouse
In which I was led.

O Suburbia!
O Suburbia!
Take away the pain
Of those children
Who cling to you
As if you were the mother
That they did not lose to work
And the misery

That seems to be a requirement for the job.

O Suburbia!

O Suburbia!

O Suburbia.

Better to Walk

When did magic go from being a legitimate explanation

To a sarcastic one?

And where was I that I never noticed?

When did spinning around in circles until we were dizzy

Turn into trying to get as fucked up as we could on as many substances as we could?

How long ago was it that that piece of rusted metal in the junkyard

Was a glimmering, cherry red marvel of human engineering?

Where was I when the spring turned to bitter winter

And the cold froze off my fingers

And I couldn't feel my throat?

Where was I

When my toy cars grew exponentially

And I could actually drive them?

And why, whenever I get down on one knee and tie my shoe in less than ten seconds
Is nobody impressed in the slightest?

How many times did I try and learn to walk before I finally got it right?
And when did that turn into a run?
And how many times did I have to fall over
And coddle scraped knees
Before I learned that sometimes, it's better to walk?

Nothing Ever Dies

Let's pretend for a minute
That no one here has to die.
That nothing ever ends.
It just keeps going and going and going
And never gets tired.
It never loses hope.

It holds on tightly
To old dreams
Older than the air we breathe
And never lets go
Even though the wind keeps attempting
To whip them from its fingers,
It, being we,
Dig ourselves deep into its core

As if to say

"If you're taking this, you gotta take us with it.

And trust us, you don't want anything to do with that."

Let's pretend for a minute

Like there's no such thing as change

And as there are no more endings

There are no more beginnings

Nothing left to learn.

Nothing left to love.

We become stuck

In perpetual mediocrity

But our apathy won't let us feel it

And so we never even know it.

We're not even moved by death any more.

It just doesn't even exist.

Can we establish here

For a second

What it is that makes someone human?

Because for me,

It's my compulsive need

To fix my fitted sheets

When they get a little bit ruffled.

Or my terrible

Inability to fall asleep

When I become even a little bit troubled.

But, that's what I get

For being such a little bitch.

And I should probably suck it up

But, I probably never will

And that's alright with me.

You will never appreciate the sober mind

Until you've been absolutely sure

That you've lost it forever.

So, let's pretend here

For one moment,

For one, small second,

That nothing ever dies

And our love moves

In beginningless

And thus,

Endless cycles

From which

We gain

Our freedom.

From which we gain our life.

Godspeak Godsend

My lungs are filled with sand

And they're weighing me down

More than you'll ever know.

Or maybe you do

And I'm just talking out of my ass.

Which, in all likelihood,

Is the case

So, from this point, I digress.

My legs are filled with jelly

And no matter how hard you push

Like a weeble

I will wobble

But I won't fall down.

My fingers are silver icicles

And when you apply enough heat

They will melt

And drip down my arms

Forming puddles at my feet

Where whales and tad poles alike

May swim until eternity

Or at least until they drown

You have skin like lavender and chamomile

You have a stomach like tungsten

And heart like steel

Like a nineteenth century factory

You are cruel and tireless

Entire movements have born to defame your name

And give the rest of us a little bit of relief.

You know, God once spoke to me

Or at least

I think it was him.

And as an atheist

I was a bit bewildered

But I listened up any way

Because I wasn't doing anything else with my day

And it really seemed like he had something important to say

So I shut up

And I listened.

I listened for hours.

I listened for days.

I listened for years.

I listened for centuries.

And by the time he was done speaking,

I was tired and old

Hungry and cold

The wind was abusing me
Like a drunk father to his son.
Violent,
Yet oddly paternal.

And if you would like to know what he said to me
To this day
I cannot say
Because when looking back,
I'm fairly certain
That he never said a thing.
He never said a thing.

You know,
We've spent the last two-thousand years or so
Making gods out of men.
I'd like to spend the next few centuries making men out of gods
  And though my lungs are filled with sand and my legs with jelly
  No matter how hard you push or pull, I will not fall
Despite my unfavorable odds.

Simple

It's all

So simple,

Really.

It's all

So simple.

It's all

So painfully,

So mind-numbingly,

So down right

Stupefyingly

Simple.

It's so simple

Just to walk

On someone's feet

When you're all

Mish-mashed together

On a busy

City street,

Crushing their toes

And laughing

Not so silently

When they cry out

In pain.

It's so simple

To sit

Between houses

In the disgusting,

Wet grass

And look

Up at the moon and notice,

Almost cynically,

How,

In your suburban cage,

The stars have all fled

To some other

Undisclosed

Place in the universe

For fear

Of being stuck

In the same

Sheltered,

Plastic and pristine

Shit hole

In which you find yourself

Now.

It's so simple

To get lost

In futile pursuits

Of lofty

Intellectualism

And sincerity

And to forget

Quite nearly

All the time

That you yourself

Are made

Of just as much

Steaming

Bull shit

As everyone else.

It's so simple

To fear

The love

You owe yourself

For all

Of the undying

Indifference

You've inflicted

Upon

Your so very weary

(World weary

Although you are young)

Heart.

It's so simple

To love

The hate

You've thrown yourself to

In an attempt

To remain

Grounded,

Which ended up

Cynical.

It's so simple

To loathe

The art

You can never make

Or understand

And walk into

Museums

With a bucket

Of red paint

To splash

And splatter

On all the paintings

And sculptures

That used to

Stare

At you

So condescendingly

From the comfort

Of their frames

And marble

Pedestals.

It's so simple

To spend

Your nights

Alone

But for

A bottle of Jack,

A pack of cigarettes,

And, maybe,

Perhaps,

A bag of marijuana

To keep you high

And satisfied

With yourself

Until

Day-break.

It's so simple

To love

love

love

And be loved

In return

Even though

The both of you know

That,

As a tragic result

Of your young age,

You were never
Meant to last.

It's so simple
To miss the things
That used to have you.

But sometimes,
On cold,
Still
Middle American nights,
When the full moon
Has fixed itself
At just the perfect angle,
And its dim,
Silver light
Hits everything
Just right,
You can see
All these things
And so much more.
And you can hear
The whispers

And shouts

And lonely moans

Of every

Simple soul

In the whole

Of simple America

And realize

That you

Are simple

Too.

Free, But Forgotten

I see it in their eyes,

A mad sort

Of restlessness,

A mad sort

Of immersion

In pixels

Blaring bright

And quick,

An ADHD genius

Destroyed by constant

Motion.

There is
A growing feeling
A sensibility,
A crippling apprehension,
A yearning
To define our youth
Using words
Our fathers used
To define themselves.

And from this,
We derive such
Lonely sadness
At our inability
To fully connect,
Make eye contact,
Breathe at the same rate,
Adopt a different tone,
Make jazz in conversation,
Spit sounds
Back and forth

Like verbal ping-pong
Risking the chance
That the ball may
Bounce up
And hit you
In your eye.

The arrogance,
The complete
And utter
Self absorption
That comes
With perpetual isolation,
A life behind
The screen.

Never before
Has a whole generation
Of people
Been so connected
And disconnected
All
At the same time.

A whole generation

Scribbling

Poetic manifestos

In spiral notebooks

Which will degrade

And tatter

As time moves on.

Brilliant!

It makes me jump for joy!

It makes me sing with passion!

And,

As the candle we use

To show the way

Begins to dwindle,

It will look

Like the flickering

Blue light

Of a computer screen

And I will dance madly

Around it

Like an apocalyptic prophet

Finally witnessing
The world
Come to its end.

Never before
Has a whole generation
Of people
Been so passionately
Apathetic.
So quick to anger,
So slow to act.
So escapist by nature,
So taken by fact.

A millenia,
A whole millenia
Of progress
Conglomerating
On this one point,
The tip
Of a wooden pencil
Making marks
On blank pages,

Scratching gibberish
And nothing
And everything.

Oh, how I yearn
To love fully
And truly
And hate fully
And truly
And watch
Patterns of light
Come together
To form images
Of things
So impossibly far away.

I want
To embrace everything
Our time
Has to offer,
Let it engulf me
In sorrow
In joy

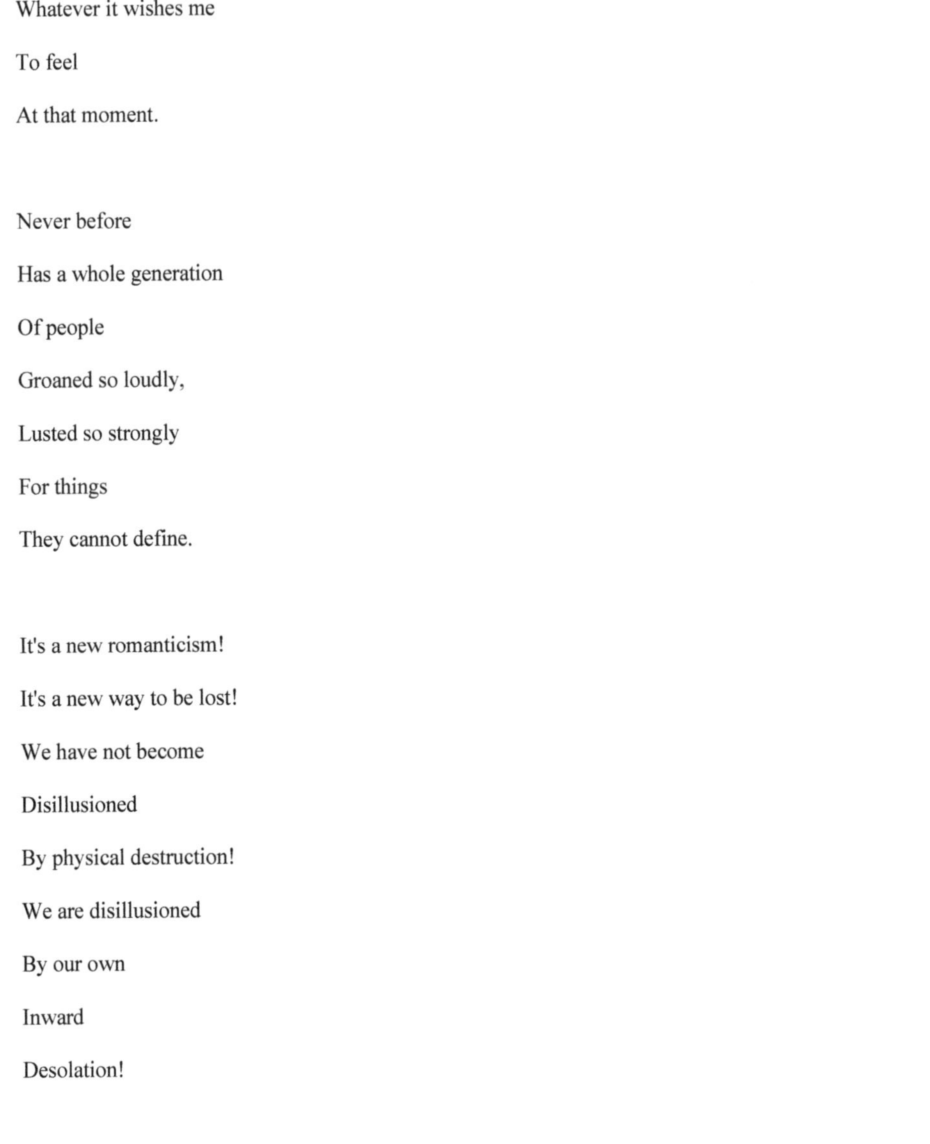

In loneliness
In excitement,
Whatever it wishes me
To feel
At that moment.

Never before
Has a whole generation
Of people
Groaned so loudly,
Lusted so strongly
For things
They cannot define.

It's a new romanticism!
It's a new way to be lost!
We have not become
Disillusioned
By physical destruction!
We are disillusioned
By our own
Inward
Desolation!

We've given up

On sincerity;

It does not exist!

We've given up

On absurdity;

It's such a given

It needs no further

Discussion!

We're jittery,

I'm jittery,

Looking for an answer

That's all our own.

But, just like

Every single generation

Before us,

We will fall short

Just as we're about

To find it.

And we know this,

I think.

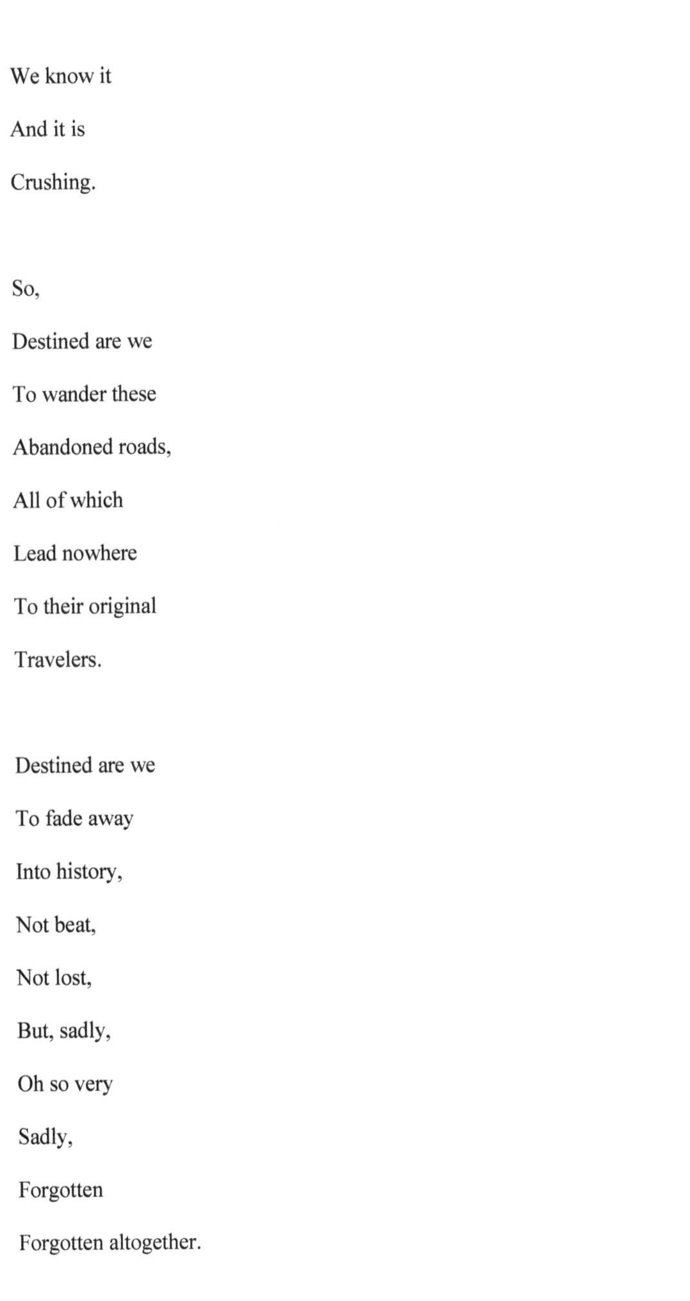

We know it
And it is
Crushing.

So,
Destined are we
To wander these
Abandoned roads,
All of which
Lead nowhere
To their original
Travelers.

Destined are we
To fade away
Into history,
Not beat,
Not lost,
But, sadly,
Oh so very
Sadly,
Forgotten
Forgotten altogether.

So,

When I look

At my life

And the things

That I've done

And the people I knew

And the things that I said

And the things that I loved

And the things that I loathed

And the music I've made

And the poems I've read

And the ground that I've walked

And the fire

That used to burn

So brightly

Over the horizon

But now is gone,

I remember

That all we would do

Is for naught.

And I am free for it.

Pop

I need more air in my tire

Before,

As I'm driving,

It pops,

Explodes rather,

And I go hurling

Across the highway

And flip

Over some side rail

Or pot hole

In the road.

Maybe

My car will be shredded

And I

Will be caught

By the tearing metal

And cut

Into a billion

Tiny,

Bloody

Pieces

Completely unrecognizable

To anyone

Who comes to my aid.

Maybe
I'll go flying
Through my wind shield
Or open window
To soar
Across the open road,
Looking down
At the eyes
Below me
As they gaze
In horror
And in wonder
At the beautiful
Bird of death
Which glides
And crashes
And crumples
Into a lifeless heap
Mere seconds
Later.

Either way,
The ground

Will be painted
A glorious,
Blood red
Mona Lisa masterpiece
The likes of which
The world has only seen
In its most
Beautiful nightmares.

And who will sing?
Who will write the poem
To accompany
This most grim art?
Who will celebrate it
In any other way
Than obligatory condolences
To the artists family?

Who will be the man
Or woman
Tasked with wiping
This piece of pop culture
History
From the face
Of this earthy canvas?

Of course,

It is also

Very possible

That the tire may pop

And I will pull over,

Replace it with a spare

And spend

Eighty bucks

On a new one,

Causing just a minor

Inconvenience

Which can be dealt with

In less

Than a day.

Shit,

I really need to change my tire.

The Table in the Woods

A table sits

Alone

In a clearing in the woods

At night.

Its marble

Corners

Have twisted

And turned

Into brilliant

White

Spires.

Leaves

Sit scattered

And aloof

Not for lack of care,

But for lack of knowledge.

They fell

From branches

Of trees

Which were sitting sadly
In the wind.

And off they went,
Floating gently
Down,
One by one,
In a nonsensical
Haze.

They landed
With barely
Even a small
Tap.

Dirt is smudged,
Making slightly brown
Its otherwise milky white
Surface
From years of disuse.

The dirt was taken
There against its will,

Another victim

Of the ever imposing

Western wind.

In the distance

There is a light,

A light

From the town

Which sits

Just outside the woods.

The town

Is quiet.

Everyone is inside,

Shut in.

The ultimate oppression

Sounds less like goosesteps

And more like silence.

The table

Sits like a weight

On light

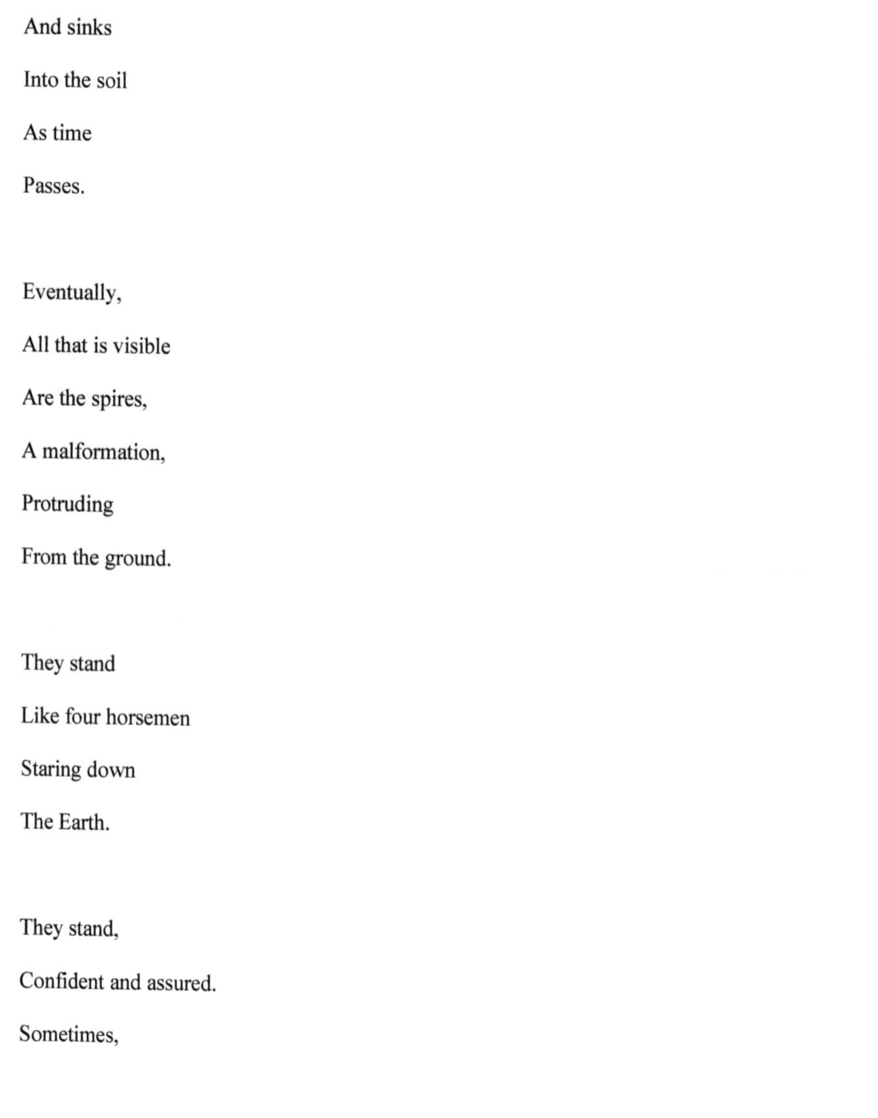

Places.

It sinks
And sinks
Into the soil
As time
Passes.

Eventually,
All that is visible
Are the spires,
A malformation,
Protruding
From the ground.

They stand
Like four horsemen
Staring down
The Earth.

They stand,
Confident and assured.
Sometimes,

It even sounds like they're laughing.

Short Stories

The First Timer

For years now, he had been practicing on his pillow. Any time he felt the blood pump from his heart to fill his shaft, he would mount his pillow like an amorous puppy and thrust away until finish. He had perfected his technique. He could fuck that pillow in any position he wanted like a pro. He could fuck it missionary, but, eventually, that got boring, so he would bend it over his bed and fuck it doggy style, just like he had seen in the movies. If he were to ever get the chance to show off his skills to an actual woman, that woman would cum so quick, she would throw him out of the room before he ever got to finish in sheer, overwhelming ecstasy.

Her hand was soft like a mother's lullaby, but her grasp was cold and indifferent. His palm was clammy and his grip clearly anxious as he was led up the stairs. With each successive step, his heart beat rose with their altitude. The music from the party seemed to mimic his anxiety in tempo. She was drunk and stumbling. He was painfully sober. He almost felt guilty as he felt he was taking advantage, but he settled his gut by telling himself that he wished he was as drunk as her and she would have done the same as she is now, regardless of sobriety. Once they reached the top of the stairs, she stumbled miserably and tripped.

He helped her stand. "Are you alright?" He asked in the most sincere sweetness he could muster, which doesn't say much.

She ignored his question and kept clumsily moving toward the bedroom door. When she finally made it, she stepped to the side and stared at him blankly to open it. He moved quickly, not wanting to disappoint, and opened the door hesitantly. Before he could step inside though, she strolled into the room and sat on the bed, facing him.

"So are you going to fuck me, or what?" She slurred, absolutely devoid of any sense of sanctity. Was she unaware that it was his first time? Was she too drunk to care? Would it be any different if she were sober? The urge to turn and leave the room nagged at him like hunger pangs to a man stranded in the desert, but, out of fear of ridicule and embarrassment, he closed the door behind him and looked in her direction.

"Of course." He managed to utter. "And I'm going to fuck you real good with...my…hard c-cock." He felt like an idiot. There was an uncomfortable silence between the two for what seemed like an eternity.

He flicked off the lights. "No! Keep them on!" She drunkenly demanded.

He obeyed immediately and watched her barely concealed breasts heave in inebriated breathlessness as he pushed forward to the bed. As he got closer, she moved further and further up the bed in anticipation of his inexperienced love. He crawled toward her and when he finally lay on top of her, kissed her gently on her lips. After the first kiss, she sloppily dove her tongue into his mouth. Saliva seemed to drench his whole face as her tongue repeatedly abandoned the companionship of his own to drunkenly move out of the confines of his mouth and explore the areas immediately surrounding it.

She lazily pushed him off of her and took his shirt off for him. She then peeled her own shirt off and unhooked her bra. "You look so beautiful…" He told her sincerely.

Without a response, as if he never said a thing at all, she pushed him backwards so he lay on his back. She undid his button and reached for the zipper. He grabbed her hand and looked down at her. She looked up at him with glazed, unfeeling eyes that seemed to say "you fucking loser." He wanted so badly to tell her to stop right there, but, instead, he pushed her hand toward her as she still gripped his zipper to help her open Pandora's Box. Next to go were his boxers, and he was left, naked and scared in front of her. She took his erect dick into her mouth and began moving her head up and down, lightly sucking. Her teeth grazed the body too many times to count, causing excruciating pain. He was screaming on the inside. Why was he here? To get his dick wet? To use this living, thinking person as a slab of meat made to be fucked by his amateur dick? His stomach was lurching as if it was taunting him, teasing him with the idea that he may vomit and ruin the whole experience for both of them. He just wanted to go downstairs and hang out with his friends. After he couldn't stand it anymore, he pushed her off of him with an almost desperate demand to stop.

Trying to save face, he lied. "I just think…that… it's about time that I do the same for you."

She nodded as if she had been thinking the same the whole time. She lay on her back and stared at him expectedly. He just looked at her, waiting for her to take her pants off, but she never did. "Well." She slurred. "Are you going to eat me out?"

Finally getting the hint, he reached forward and unbuttoned her. When he reached for her zipper, she grabbed his hand as if she wanted him to stop. Elated, he looked to her expecting for his nightmare to end. He was met with a sharp, mocking laugh, and it was made clear to him that she was only poking fun at him as she pushed his hand down in the same way he had done earlier. Trembling, he pulled her pants down and did the same to her panties. She was barely moist, and her vagina was perfectly pink and shaved so finely as if it had been waxed specifically for occasions like these.

He pressed his lips to hers and began flicking his tongue awkwardly. It was salty and bitter like a rotten strawberry, and he couldn't make up his mind whether or not he liked the taste. Occasionally, he would look to her face to see how she was enjoying herself, as he couldn't hear her over the sound of his inward meltdown. Her face was as blank as ever, only this time, it looked as if she was waiting bored at a bus stop for her ride to come. He kept going though, thinking that the longer he kept at it, the more likely it would be that he find a spot that works. He searched everywhere, but could not find any success and eventually lifted his head to show that he was done trying.

“Do you have any condoms?” She asked like a strict school teacher asks a student if he’s got his homework.

“Uh, no. I mean, I wasn’t –“

“Fuck it. I don’t care.” He wasn’t surprised. “Just fuck me.”

He looked at her, half terrified, half exhilarated, and prepared himself to enter her womanhood. Much to his dismay, he couldn’t seem to do so. He couldn’t stop thinking. He could never stop thinking. What if, when he’s fucking her, he goes limp and his very masculinity is called into question? What if he gets her pregnant? What if this was nothing like fucking his old pillow back home? What if? His heart was racing faster than ever. His body was perspiring all over. He felt like he had just run a marathon, and he hadn’t even started fucking her yet. The words “No. I’m sorry, I can’t do this” sat like a stone in the middle of his throat and he found it nigh impossible to breathe. For his whole life, he envisioned himself as a sexual king. He thought he would be the kind of man that had women groveling at his feet for his master phallus. Now that he was finally here, where he had wanted to be for so long, he found it so meaningless and dissatisfying. He had decided that this was not the way he wanted to give up his virginity. He now found himself dreaming of tender kisses and whispers of love in the dark. He wanted to cuddle and laugh with his partner who would love him just as much as he loved her. He wanted to go back so badly, but he had already gone too far. To go back now would be an unforgivable insult to everyone from this girl whom he was using to his friends who relentlessly pushed him into taking her hand. He had to do it. He had to do it now.

He pushed his pelvis forward and entered her warm body. He began to move in and out of her as he supported his upper body with violently shaking arms. She felt amazing, but he found no signs of pleasure in her face. It almost looked to him like she was falling deeper asleep with each thrust. As he examined the situation to see what exactly he was doing wrong, he realized that his thrusts were really just awkward and frantic flails like he was hemorrhaging from bleeding of the heart. He was terrible and he knew it.

He finished up quickly and pushed himself from off of her. Without a word from either of them, they both put their clothes back on. She left the room before he had even finished pulling his pants up and he was all alone. Just as he felt he always would be for the rest of his days. Destined was he to forever find vixens like her, girls pretty enough to love fully, but hollow and cold enough to never reciprocate. Women who have loved and been hurt so many times that once they stumble upon a boy so naïve and inexperienced as he, all he can do is make them sick and more cynical. The only way to ever fully know them would be to disconnect himself from all warmth as they have, and live for eternity in a frozen tundra of emotion, and, although the thought drained him of all hope and happiness, he knew it was inevitable. He walked home alone that night. He walked home alone like he knew he would for the rest of his days, telling himself all the while “You did it. You’re a man now.”

A Walk Through Suburbia

What is the sky but a vast expanse of nothing? Perhaps one will find clusters of water vapor clumped together to form domineering figures that look like whatever it is that the imagination wants them to look like, but, for the most part, there is nothing. It's amazing how beautiful nothing can seem.

What is it that drives people to disrupt such beauty? Houses, man made of course, obstruct my view of the canvas above me. Below me is not much better. The grass and its warm, friendly green has been removed and replaced by the hard, gray, apathetic face of concrete. The summer heat only makes it worse. I'm no longer walking along a side walk; rather, a more suitable term may be griddle. I should have worn shoes. No, I'm actually quite glad that I chose to travel bare foot. It's the most dangerous thing I'll do all day.

Row upon seemingly endless row of almost identical houses consume the environment. At around five or six o' clock, thousands of men rush home from jobs they hate to eat mediocre, microwavable meals and ignore a family that they don't really cherish. Afterwards, they'll knock back a few beers and get so drunk that they've forgotten that their surroundings are entirely synthetic. The next day, they'll wake with a debilitating hang over and go on hating their lives and regretting their past. Welcome to Suburbia: where the soul goes to die.

*　　　*　　　*

'Here you go, man." Hernando's smile is a favorite of mine.

I pull the money from my pocket and make the exchange. It's disgusting that I have to pay for my soul in such a secretive, under handed way, but I find comfort in the fact that my money is directly responsible for helping him support his daughter. Hernando is a short Hispanic man of the same age as me, with a shaven head and light facial hair, whose eyes always twinkled with a spirit that I envied. I imagine it stems from his child. I don't think he chose to have a daughter so young, but I'm glad he did. Older men squandered their youths and lost sight of what really mattered until they had children, but by then, it was too late. Their upbringings had taught them wrong in the most important time of their lives, and they suffered as adults for it. Hernando had the luxury of learning early. I know that no matter where life takes him, he will always have that twinkle in his eye. He is beautiful and always will be.

I continue on my way. I stop briefly at the park. I have to cut my visit short as a cop car pulls into the parking lot. I find it absurd that I have to scramble so frantically to cover up my completely victimless crime, but I figure that now isn't the time to practice civil disobedience. Hand cuffs hurt.

I hate this place. I hate it like I've never hated anything before in my entire life. This sort of life that they (you ask me who "they" is and I don't even have an answer, which makes it that much worse) have provided for me does nothing for the soul. There is no danger. There is nothing to work for besides arbitrary societal expectations like making the best grades or preserving the status quo. Every single goal that we all stress ourselves so heavily for is entirely man made, and yet, we treat it as if Mother Nature herself demanded it from us. I frequently observe my peers at school, watching them scramble to finish work for classes they hate only because they want that specific class rank and to get into the best school so they could have the best career and the best life. I'm disgusted. I'd like to see them take all those accomplishments to the grave.

I apparently haven't been paying as much attention to where I am walking as I should be. I fail to see a wasp on the ground just where my foot is about to land. It stings me in my toe. I scream expletives at a little girl who just so happened to be wandering by. Obviously frightened, she quickens her pace to distance herself from me. I don't know whether I am satisfied with myself, or disappointed, or even if I care enough to make that distinction. I enjoy providing the eccentricity for this god forsaken, soulless wasteland. I feel it benefits other people as much as it benefits me. That little girl just felt something real. She felt terror. She could see the pain and hatred in my eyes. She knows now that there is more to life than the thoughtless, plastic coating that she's always been too ignorant, or perhaps even afraid to acknowledge. I have given her the chance to grow up and be as miserable here as I am.

My walk has morphed into a limp. My foot is throbbing. I would like to go home. I feel a creeping sickness in my belly. My mouth is dry. I'm miserable. I trip over my feet. My head hits the concrete. There is no one around to help me off of the ground. I lay there, in more pain than I have been in a very long while, looking up at the emptiness above me. This time, I say nothing. I just watch the clouds hover above me, laughing at me from their impossibly high homes in the sky. As I watch, the clouds take on various shapes. One resembles a rhino preparing itself to charge. Another, a face laughing at some outrageously hilarious joke that I would give anything to hear. I know they aren't really there, but that's the art, the beauty of it all. I find it amazing that one can make such vivid realities out of otherwise dull and meaningless blobs of vapor.

Suddenly, something clicks in my head. Thoughts of Hernando and the little girl come flooding into my awareness. Hernando is stuck in the same spot that I am, and yet, his happiness is more real than anything I could imagine. He manages to find beauty in his situation; a feat I thought impossible. And the little girl: who am I to say that she'll become miserable here? If

Hernando can find happiness, why can't she? I showed her real emotion. I showed her potential and it was hers then to do with what she wished. Perhaps my environment does lack a certain soul or a certain meaning, but all that provides is room for my own to grow. I can be happy if I truly wished to be. I can be anything at all if I really, honestly wanted it. After all, the sky is just empty space and the clouds are just clouds until you will them to be something else.

An Essay

High Time for Change

America: Land of the free, home of the brave. Our great nation provides the moral candle to illuminate the rest of the world and save them from the tyranny of communism/terrorism (really just whatever common enemy the government decides to throw at us to keep us from clamoring for their throats). One would think that in a country such as ours, personal privacy would be allowed to exist without having to be subject to the government's meddling. If I keep something to myself and never use it to harm others or strip them of their own liberties, how, in any reasonably just sense, can that activity be deemed illegal? Unfortunately, I am referencing actual laws that affect us at this very moment: American drug laws.

I myself am a victim of these heinous infringements on our individual rights. Simply for possessing a relatively minuscule amount of marijuana, I was arrested, jailed, and treated like a common criminal. Am I really such a danger to the people around me that I deserved this? I routinely scoff at those who jump to violence as their primary method of problem solving. I felt guilty for stealing a pack of Pokémon cards and have not stolen since. I am a pacifist obsessed with being the best person I can be.

I am not a criminal. And yet, I was made to feel like one.

I was released to my parents late the night of my arrest. At that point, I clung to the idea that I had broken the law and my detainment was simply a product of my arresting officer doing her job. This naive optimism was completely demolished in the few days that followed. My parents shared with me a story of a recent night on the town in which they witnessed a woman's jacket containing her cell phone stolen by some punk in front of Star bucks. As expected, the police chased after the thief, caught him, and immediately arrested him. As much as I would love for that last part to be true, it sadly cannot be further from it. Once the thief was captured, he was made to give back the stolen property and immediately released to play guitar in front of the coffee shop from whence he came. When this story was told to a friend of my parents (who also happens to be a cop), she condemned those officers for not kicking the criminal out of the area. She truly considered this proper justice.

I would hope that the flaw there demands the attention from you that it immediately did from me. This punk had engaged in an indisputably criminal act and gets treated like a toddler caught with his hand in the cookie jar.

It is high time for our current attitudes towards the consumption of mind altering substances to receive a radical change. Now, just to be clear, I am not advocating or even remotely suggesting that one take any drugs. However, I am arguing for one's right to do so and why our policies should be changed. Please know that I do acknowledge the physical draw backs of taking drugs and am also in favor of seeing a general decline in usage (particularly amongst my peers, who tend to stress their limits with these types of things).

Very possibly, the best way to ensure that these unjust occurrences never afflict another innocent soul would be to change the legal status of these drugs, and make them legal. 'Well, that's just a given!' you may find yourself rolling your eyes and shouting at me (which would be a most odd reaction as I probably happen to be nowhere near you at this very moment), but, do not be disillusioned just yet, for that represents only the tip of the ice berg.

I would first like to address this proposition by taking a look at its opposition. Perhaps the most compelling argument against drug legalization refers to the economic impacts of such a radical change. It's been suggested that the making legal of currently illegal drugs may lead to more drug related health concerns which will ultimately be paid for by tax payers. This is a valid point.

Drug legalization may very well demand more money from our pockets, but there certainly exist some measures we can take to make sure this is not entirely the case. Of course, one solution would be to simply eliminate some already existing taxes that we feel unnecessary, and keep our rates at relatively the same levels they exist at currently. The problem with this proposition however, lies in the fact that it ignores the very purpose of taxation in the first place. To eliminate certain taxes all together would deplete funding for the services they support, and those services would inevitably disappear.

It would seem that the most effective way to answer these economic questions would be to impose a sort of sin tax on drugs. In other words, the substances in question may be taxed fairly heavily so as to collect enough revenue to cover these health care costs. The consumers would then carry the burden of their own health care costs, relieving the pockets of those who do not wish to partake in the same activities. Even if proven incorrect, the exterior costs would be just grounds for discouraging drug use, not making it illegal.

What the issue ultimately and inevitably comes down to is a debate over whether or not we as humans possess the right to consume whatever drug we want. The simplest answer to this question is yes. Yes we do. The issue quite easily exceeds the limits of economic questions and finds itself in the murky waters of actual criminal behavior and a general moral objection to the use of currently illegal drugs in any context.

Currently, the government approaches their drug policy with the intent to prevent crime. It is no secret that certain drugs have a tendency to increase aggressive attitudes and, in some cases, completely dissociate their user from normal reality and plant them in some alternate universe. What the government fails to acknowledge with this approach is the subjectivity of the effects a drug user experiences. Bob Everyman may have raped his girlfriend while under the influence of PCP, but Joe Six-pack has taken PCP multiple times without harming a single soul. Bob deserves to be arrested and tried because he raped his girlfriend, not for taking the drug. It is far more reasonable to arrest drug users for the actual harm they do to others, rather than the potential harm they might do.

The morality argument suffers the same flaw. By justifying the war on drugs as a sort of moral crusade, the subjectivity of morality gets ignored. The morality argument seems to suggest that there exists an objective morality that we must adhere to in every scenario. While perhaps that may hold true in cases as severe as murder, there exist certain acceptable situations in which killing another human being becomes accepted (or, in some cases, expected). Morality is specific to the individual, and for one to impose their version on another person, the imposer has claimed their morality the better morality (otherwise, why would they be imposing in the first place?), and the subjectivity of moral codes would dictate that there exists no such thing as a superior morality. In other words, if I take no issue with risking the potential health problems to get high, and my neighbor does not think that I should, I can take his suggestion if I so wish, but still retain my right to pollute my own body. The current system creates that same picture, although the neighbor, instead of merely suggesting, barges into my home, strips me of my drugs, throws me in jail, and forces me to pay him a large sum of money simply because he did not like what I happened to be doing to myself.

Millions of innocent drug users find themselves in handcuffs every day simply for possessing just about any amount of psychoactive substance. Devoted pacifists are lumped together with ravenous killers for the sole reason that they happened to possess a consumable amount of marijuana. Quite clearly, a change needs to take place in the ways our government approaches the topic of drugs. Innocent people have been made to suffer for far too long, they have just been too out of it to notice.

www.ingramcontent.com/pod-product-compliance
Ingram Content Group UK Ltd.
Pitfield, Milton Keynes, MK11 3LW, UK
UKHW041917190726
13854UKWH00003B/1295

9 781105 592638